The Blocked Heart

Also by Edwin Brock

Invisibility Is the Art of Survival
Paroxisms
The Portraits & The Poses

The
Blocked
Heart

Edwin Brock

A New Directions Book

ACKNOWLEDGMENTS
Grateful acknowledgment is made to the editors and publishers of books and magazines in which some of the poems in this volume first appeared: *Ambit, Antaeus, Atlantic Monthly, New Directions in Prose and Poetry 31*, and *Southern Review*.

Manufactured in the United States of America
First published clothbound and as New Directions Paperbook 399 in 1976
Published simultaneously in Canada by McClelland & Stewart, Ltd.

Library of Congress Cataloging in Publication Data

Brock, Edwin.
  The blocked heart.

  (A New Directions Book)
  I. Title.
PR6003.R38723B5   821'.9'14   75–6528
ISBN 0–8112–0577–0
ISBN 0–8112–0578–9 pbk.

New Directions Books are published for James Laughlin
by New Directions Publishing Corporation,
333 Sixth Avenue, New York 10014

For James Laughlin

Contents

Death in November 1
FIVE WAYS TO KILL A BATTERY HEN 2
Paterfamilias 7
In memory of B. S. Johnson 8
Nearer, my God! 9
Sunday morning 11
The Bonsai poem 12
A fresh start 13
Hurry up please its time 15
ALL THE WORLD'S A STAGE
1. Rehearsal 18
2. When the music stops 19
3. Thy neighbour 21
4. Or would you rather scream? 22
5. All the world's a stage 24
Formula for success 26
The offering 28
MARKET OPPORTUNITY 30
An enquiry into the nature of things 35
The genius of John Cannell 37
Diagnosis 38
Just before Christmas 39
BEACH POEMS 41
November 44
Risen sparrow 45
Pastoral 46
Monkey Puzzle 46
A late Valentine for Liz 48
THREE POSITIONS
1. The chair position 49
2. The couch position 50
3. The bird position 50
Inheritance 52
Vocations 53
Nursery rhyme 54

Death in November
(In memory of Matthew Brock)

Month of the dead fly,
and maggots dormant in stiff grass

month of the burned guy,
abandoned nests and iron frost

month when the old year
twists itself upon young throats

cold of the hanged year and
Christmas lights switched on by ghosts

when death, too much for tiny shoulders,
suffocates a son who leaves
singing in the early morning
and prayer before sleep

who made even suffering seem boy-size
by telling in a two-year voice
dwarfing grief we make enormous
to fill a lifetime's loss

whose memory makes us regret
the intellect that breaks belief:
today we threw a Christmas toy away
and bought a wreath.

FIVE WAYS TO KILL A BATTERY HEN
(For Henry Graham)

One.

She was not made for this:
her lungs are not large enough
for these gusts
and one by one feathers
fly from her yellow flesh

alone on the only hill in Norfolk
she waits for the end when
like Elijah's chariot
a whirlwind will take her up
and like the burned boy drop her
in the middle of a marsh mist

her eyes are shut and she is dreaming
of steel gates closing over Europe:
of daily medication, balanced grain
eat and produce, eat and produce

in those days her Eden
was the one hill in a garden
of manageable dangers,
now she would change the world
to dream behind bars
of this murderous freedom.

---

* See page 56 for an explanatory note on 'Five Ways to Kill a Battery Hen.'

Two.

We did it in the yard
of a London police station:

we drew a circle in the dust
with a chicken's beak and
dumped the creature in the middle
of its own circumference

we watched it walk
again and again to the dirt furrow
and return defeated to the centre

then, when the drunks had
stopped singing, we unlocked
the cells and walked away;
by morning they were empty

we waited until the sun's first rays
filled the hen's circle
then we pulled its neck
and threw the body into an empty cell

we saw, as the carcass cooled
on the cell's stone floor,
the fleas leave their sinking ship
but we never saw our prisoners again.

Three.

The fields are heavy on my head
the sun is heavy on the fields
and this is the first harvest.

The soil is soft, it takes my claws
like a rich man's carpet
where I am feeding on the world.

That spot on the sun is of no
significance, there is too much sun
around it: it is a little shade.

I am alive in this shade; I am
alone in the shade; the
shade is a shadow. Only

I am in the shadow; why
am I alone in the shadow?
why is there a red pain

here? Why am I
a red pain screaming in a small shadow?
and why has the screaming stopped?

Four.

The hen in my pocket
is no longer a party-piece:
the days when Brock's hen
tugged its leash in traffic
or clucked eggs in
crowded pubs have gone

The hen in my pocket
does not pose for photographs:
mostly she sleeps in darkness
with her feathers flat
and her beak
pecking pocket fluff

The hen in my pocket
cannot hear my friends:
she has forgotten when
it was appropriate
for an advertising poet
to go to work on an egg

Today my pocket stinks
of dying. I blame the bird
and the bird blames me.
There is no reality:
neither knows
what each proposed
to the other.

Five.

You are no ordinary hen:
I made you out of old timetables
and Christmas decorations;
I made you out of Mulligan's
nights of the turntable,
a London wind and the two children
of a broken marriage. Hen,
I made you out of needing you.

Dull hills with sheep on them
were going nowhere; a damp
blanket of fog was rotting
apples and bruised plums;
every log was alive with beetles
and centipedes, and whisps of black hair
blew across my mouth whenever
the wind was in that direction.

I made you in a shed with high nettles
among mildewed trees: there
was very little truth in you;
I showed you off and you grew
oversize from too much attention:
almost you became a nightmare.

Hen, I have stopped dreaming you now:
the doctors say this therapy
is too little and too late. I remember
a Tibetan thought-form which grew
thin and ugly as its maker tired.
The remedy is isolation: you and I
must stare each other out. Open
your eyes, hen, look at me and shout.

Paterfamilias

This deep sepia
matches exactly
the rough red Victorian covering
and the brown vase
with a picture
of someone scattering something

mathematically head-on
and almost lifesize
both eyes dominate the room
like a poster of Kitchener

with a duelling scar
the long jaw
could pass easily for Prussian,
and five feet below the frame
the legs may enter
jackboots or
Bond Street leather

no doubt pierces
its paper eyes,
for centuries
they have stared over guns
sure of only one thing:
that orders are made
to be obeyed

in boyhood
I prayed upwards
to this familiar cruelty,
now on a level
with my own eyes
I scrape its history
every day.

In memory of B. S. Johnson

My neighbour's eye
makes his window
an opaque pond

beneath the surface
screams start
and break like gas bubbles.

On Winterton sands
seabirds scream and dive
as I pass their nests

on their doorstep
the big fish swim
with their mouths open.

I am drinking in
a London pub with
a poet whose name blinks
from the obituaries

gossip puts him together again
in a locked house
in a warm bath
in blood and water.

Between these things
the earth is extinguished
between these things
the days are
counted and rationed
like bought love.

Little wonder
that in this calendar
I make ponds
where screams rise
like gas bubbles

Little wonder
I make an eye
where each fish
is a mouth opening
on zig-zag birds.

These are things
I make to make myself

but the poet
makes himself for me
and I am still running.

Nearer, my God!

Stand
in the middle
of the Acle Straight
and spin:

if you could paint this
the horizon would be
two inches from
the bottom of the paper,
the rest would be sky.

Take
one field,
green on its side
like a Matisse table

and find in the middle
of a flush of spring grass
the liver fluke.

It is waiting
to be eaten
to crawl inside a cow
to lay its eggs
in the red liver
to leave chewing offspring
to be pancaked
in the new grass
to make a meal
for a cow.

If that cow
stood in this field
and turned

the horizon would be
ruler-straight and low
under a maximum sky.

The cow
need not necessarily die
of parasites

sometimes
it has other ends.

Reading this
in the middle
of the Acle Straight
my wife asks
if she can help me

and this question
in a country of such low horizons
frightens.

Sunday morning

The appetite of God!
think of a bird
stuffed in a bird
inside a pig's mouth
on a warm plate.

Think of the world
gathering weight
from its own intestine!

There is so little space,
perhaps enough for
a thrifty winter,
therefore I weed my head
making room for Mozart
intending to go down fighting.

A heron stands over
this river, pointed out
by weekend cruisers
and swans waiting for
sliced bread and cake.

Even here men knock
and ask questions: am I
ready to meet my maker?
do I copulate
with the earth?

Creation is eating madness,
only space is indigestible,
therefore I stay thin inside
quiet at the sea's edge
looking back to the beginning
disguised as nothing, thinking
like a chameleon on fire.

The Bonsai poem

If you take an acorn
and plant it in
a small container
with a drainage hole,
you may train the seedling
into a gnarled oak
only ten inches high

this is done by
leaf-stripping
shoot-pinching
and lifting the tree
from its bed each winter
to trim the roots

by the careful choice
of container and
a thoughtful use
of stone and moss
you strive for a strained
look, a tortured look
the look of a tree
which has fought its environment
for a nightmare survival

you may attain
in ten years or so
the ravages of a century:
summers of lightning
winters of hard frost
and the burning
of a salt-sharp wind

yet all the time
your oak has been screened
in a formal garden
syringed in summer and
pruned with fine polished knives

half closing your eyes
you may one day dream yourself
into its shade
having found it suffering
in some god-forsaken
corner of England

and if when your dream ends
you find yourself
in proportion to the old-young tree
in some god-forsaken corner
gnarled, trimmed and ten times
your age, your years of patience
will have brought you
face to face
with the psychology of loss.

A fresh start

A potter perhaps
with his head in meditation
and his hands in health. . . .

or doing something
to huge planks
of overwhelming pine. . . .

a man of God and soil
sowing muscles
and reaping peace. . . .

'Why don't you write a bestseller?'
my daughter asks.

Such immense possibilities
that almost I am tempted
to take the glass from
my neighbour's wall and call
that I am not to be disturbed.

In this village
a girl was raped
in a riverside chalet:
a dancer with long legs
and professional breasts

all week a jury has been fed
its own handy fantasy
rewritten as a moral tale:
'Would she have done it
for me without complaint?'

Later, I am walking by the river
staring underneath tall trees
trying to discover something

a potter would not do this:
he would sit on a hillside
in Japan with his head
up God's arse, making glory.

What stupidity! I have planted
my mother in this field
in the wrong soil in the wrong season
and wonder why she does not grow!

Excuse me, a neighbour asks
it is happening again.

I cannot help her:
my mother must be resurrected
in the right place,
my wives, sons, daughters
given life. What does God
do on Sundays!

There must be a change of plan:
obviously we must move again
nothing grows here
there is too much wind
too much noise
too many neighbours
and too little rain.

Hurry up please its time

Pussy cat, pussy cat
I know London was there
for carved like a mouse
on a kitchen chair
I heard my father
across the water speak
of dogs in Club Row
whitewashed to keep
their spots from showing

Cat, my father knew London
like the back of a hand
in a backstreet pub
turned over to sell
the cracks of the Union Canal

I do not think he'd ever seen
St. Paul's, The Tower or
the Queen, and the Guards
could change to red-eyed
stoats before he'd cross
a bridge to look

He left in a stinging fog
carrying pincers and pliers
to twist together
the tattered ends
of all the City's wires,
but his goodbye was longer
than he thought and even now
we have not caught up

Cat, do you remember
when we had a King
with a Jubilee and ate tea
in the streets and ran races
and scrambled for pennies?

Do you remember when
Sunday was a noise of bells
and a one-armed rag-and-bone man
sang the same song
from Aldgate to the Old Kent Road?
What has happened since then?

His bones are on a London hill
built over by a block of flats
and that square mile
is the concrete cell
where I sat to sew bread and water

Cat, why can't God afford to live
in these churches any more?
Why does the Queen get older
all the time? Pussy cat
where have you been?
I have a mouse still waiting
to hide and a childhood
dying of nursery rhymes.

ALL THE WORLD'S A STAGE
(For Dannie Abse)

1.   Rehearsal

Nature is spiky:
the sharp grass, rushes
gorse, broom, all
thrusting up

the lady in the red hat
meanders
like music, rests
between acts
and in the corner of a field
opens her throat
and blows Mozart
without a sound

the thin moon
is colder than I remembered,
the stars
are sharp in frost:
I know I am home
and that it may snow

a small copse
of grey trees
planted in rows
each one ten feet
from the other:
if the lady walks there
there may be
no end to it

spiky Norfolk!
the sharp grass thrusting up
and this lady growing
warm arms around it

it would be hot in her
although the stars would drop
white frost upon us

this time
I think something strange
is happening

and that I have gone
over into that grey copse
again.

2.   When the music stops

There is a black crack across
the weather which will widen
as the breeze begins

all day there have been signs:
a dog crying at a door
which would not open
black spots upon the rose
and a cat which died

I have been restless:
my eyes so deep into my head
that my face was a mask
searching the trees
for something to show

in a moment the lady will knock.

I do not want to know
why the man with the red-grey face
beats his mistress until she screams
nor why this lady goes
running to the shop
for gin and contraceptives.
Excuse me, she says
but it is happening again.

The weather has turned
to rain. The low sky has blown
the green apart to show
old hiding places.
It is this moment.

Now across two fields
a stoat bars a rabbit
whose screams start before
his heart gives out. Does
the red-grey man know this?

Could I face his mistress
until she screams? Could
she run to the shop for gin?
Could the man hide in
these fields until the end?

Excuse me, she says
but it is happening again.
Sometimes I feel the clockwork
winds down more quickly
and the weather is changing
faster than it began.

3. Thy neighbour

The man has learned to play
on a cheap recorder
Over The Hills and Far Away

over and over, joining each end
to a new beginning in a flat rhythm
which tunes in epilepsy and migraine.

He is punishing us all
for the things we have taken away.

Now a bell is ringing
as though someone is unclean:
once the mould is broken
anything may happen, for no-one
is chosen, not even to be crucified.

Somewhere some dream is playing the man
as the man plays me. I do not think
he can stop blowing. I do not think
I will ever live in silence again.

Halfway to the horizon
the grass is singing
to the bell's metronome
and soon the recorder will bring
animals from the trees' shadows
dragging their shadows with them.

If I knew
what the man had lost

If I knew
why he is mourning

If I could ask him
what we have taken away

I would brave the horizon
to come back carrying it

but this sin goes back so far
not even the man remembers

and today he has found
its perfect expression

leaving us
with a new adjustment to make.

4. Or would you rather scream?

They have taken the lady away
who lay on her dry bed screaming
but the man maintains his monologue
saying
      if you lay there screaming
      they will take you away

He is red and grey and walks
ten times a day to a corner shop
for a biscuit and a piece of cheese

He dare not believe
the screaming has stopped
and coming back from the corner shop
makes a telephone call
to hear someone screaming
      If you scream all day
      they will take you away
he shouts and slams the plastic
in its quiet grave.

They have taken the lady away
and the screaming has stopped
and boredom is with us now as though
a biscuit and a piece of cheese
can satisfy a hungry soul.

The weather has dropped down again
the clouds are low and it is cold:
the man in the corner shop
has piled stock upon his counter
against the moment when
the weather breaks –
if only things were that simple.

I have been told it may be necessary
to hold one's face in
a poker mask and breathe deeply
for these things to pass
and that peace will come
slowly through the mirror

I cannot tell the man these things
I do not think I could convey
such faith
to a red-grey face

     Darling he says on the telephone
     if you stop screaming
     they'll let you come home
not knowing that what he most dreads
that break with God
will always happen.

Returning from the corner shop
he has clung to his bed
and tried to dream

but biscuits and cheese ten times a day
have kept the bogeyman away
and boredom is what happens when
the screaming stops.

I am under a freezing cloud
watching two swallows play
all day my sickness has been locked in
by thinking

If only the lady would come back again
If only the dog would stop howling
If only the cloud would lift
Darling the man says on the telephone
tomorrow everything may change

of such prayers are saints made
who see and hear and starve
and scream silently.

5. **All the world's a stage**

The lady in the red hat has seen God
you can tell by the way she speaks to no-one
and makes her mascara run;
beside her a man erects a belly dance
and does sums to split the universe.

No-one is looking at me! I would like
the lady in the hat to see my liver,
my lights and that corner of my mind
where I hide for excitement – whose turn
is it up there anyway? everyone
gets two minutes, that's in the rules!

Secretly the red-hat lady's vision comes.
It is rubbish. I tell her what I see
and she runs away. 'Look' I say
to the mathematician 'stuff your sums!'
'But it's magic' he says 'just like poetry'.

Tant pis! I'll join the man contemplating
his belly dancers. 'Unfortunately'
he says 'it is finished' and shows me
a personality as limp as wet string.

The stage manager believes we are
all mad. 'There's nothing up there'
he shouts. He stops the projector,
switches off the tape and deliberately
tunes in to silence. It is not silent:
around the sound of violins keening
I can hear the insects screaming.

A formula for success

If you put one leg
ahead of your body
balance on it and swing
the other you move
a yard forward

this takes one second
of your life.

If you put one sunrise
ahead of your vision
balance on it and swing
forward you move
into nightfall

this takes one day
of your life.

Similarly weeks
months and years
may be annihilated
with practice

until a lifetime
passes without pain.

The trick is in balance
and momentum
always keeping your eyes
on horizons and your mind
on a goal

until moving demonstrates
horizons and goals.

Mostly you will travel
through people
without contact
for contact is not
essential to progress

but in event of contact
it must be swift
heavy and irreversible
so that momentum
is not checked

this technique
once acquired
will carry you through
all institutions
whether domestic
or social.

Failures will occur
through striking others
when off balance
or catching an eye
at point of contact

this causes relationship
and breaks momentum.

Try always
to sleep deeply
and without dreaming
remembering
when dreams occur
that they have
no meaning

dress well
eat well and be
always moving
for there are horizons
everywhere
continually travelling
at your own good speed.

The offering

Imagine an elevator
rising slowly
between floors
as though it cannot arrive

imagine a
deformed child
blind behind
pink plastic eyes

I am speaking:
the child hears
my voice and makes
her face shine.

Why can I not explain
that this is mine
and that when I touch
her face it is like
arriving here?

A woman smiles
as though this
excuses her involvement

and I accept
as I accept
the dull truth
describing everything.

Waiting between floors
in the darkness
between floors
something brushes me

and I buy my daughter
a strange doll
to help her illness.

Take everything
that is offered
I advise her

as together
we kiss the twisted toy
in her warm bed.

MARKET OPPORTUNITY
(For John Miyauchi)

You do not know us.

We do not show ourselves.

But we have made you
in a profitable image.

Our wars do not concern you:
they are our wars.

Our peace-talks do not concern you:
they are ours.

You need do nothing
except eat, sleep and enjoy yourselves.

You need do nothing except
emulate your neighbours.

We have you here
in one segment or another

measured by age, by region
or by class

we have you counted
and will make predictions.

*

Forgive me
for speaking like that.

I am in an air-conditioned room
which makes my body seem obscene

outside my window
the jets fly and land silently

there is no other view.

A society of servants
pamper me for money

my private bathroom
reeks of white

and my soiled socks
insult me.

I do not sleep at night

the miners are burrowing
beneath my bed

the pharmacists
are grinding new pills

I write the spells
for this sad society

the clean and clever lad
who got on.

*

This is perhaps
my last commitment:

looking for faces
among the figures.

Ten years on
my daughter in a village school
is the new consumer.

It is either this or bombs
there is no other future.

        *

The jets fly and land silently.

Two birds abandon
the new estate.

We scrape deeper
for the sea's last fish

raping our space.

Reading this
is our entertainment.

Forgive us
for God is long since gone.

   *

We are all nice men
with wives and white teeth.

'We are proud of our computer'

I love the paunch
under the shirt
under the discreet jacket.

We have marched there and back
without Wagner
or even a drum.

We used only one
of our issued condoms
on a plain Waaf
and married her.

Now a bored girl on a white horse
pushes a button and falls
back towards another climax.

A black African watches
a metal copulation.

The machine shivers
under the cold soles of our feet.

God taught us this way
of making things.

*

In another day
I will show you something new

back from factories
and bright windows
you will believe me

for I have the last Utopia:
a bought future.

I am your needs:
I have eaten fish and chips
in Stavely and
drunk cocktails in Leeds

and inasmuch as you
will climb to heaven
on a neighbour's neck
I will sell you
spiked climbing boots.

In a corner of my grey mind
I find a kindness
for small children
and thin dogs but

you and I are too far gone:
Egypt is over
our right shoulder
and we are running south

there the air thins
in bright flat patterns
and a small child cries
in each dry dog's mouth.

An enquiry into the nature of things

I've spent the day walking through London
with a ball of string in my pocket
and the free end in my hand

a childhood book explained
that this was the proper way
to find yourself in a maze

consequently the West End, the City
and every bridge leading to Camberwell
is criss-crossed to this cold room

and in this room, rattled by branches
I sit with my head wedged
in the brickwork to keep the water out.

All these things were told me by God.

The conservationists say that there
are fish in the Thames
but do not say which fish. I know

which fish are in the Thames
the coelacanth are in the Thames gorging
on shit and wastepaper: the fish

the historians believed had died
with God, not knowing that we had
kept Him alive to explain the popsongs.

A coelacanth with one end of my
string in his spine told me this.

At night I dream I am on a shingle beach;
there is no freedom in it; my head says
this stone, that stone to where I put my feet:

in the third part of the dream I whirl
a lion around my head by his tail
to smash his eyes out on the flat stones

this way, that way says his head to my feet
this way, that way my stretched muscles repeat
this way, that way I go having learned nothing.

My mother with her head
in my mouth told me this.

I know that something is very near
understanding but I cannot smile
or feel relief. On Sunday

we take a snot-nosed mongol
to the beach: Faster, faster she sings
in the car, exploding a sausage roll

she calls strangers Daddy, kisses dogs
and is as insane as a fourteen-year-old
body in a four-year-old brain.

I chant the Old Man from Penang
whose bollocks went off with a bang;
I tie string around the lion's eyeballs,

the mongol's nose and my mother's throat
and, following the coelacanth along
the shitbed of the Thames, shout

Faster, faster, not caring where we go.
Something is very near understanding.
And my family of mutant offspring told me this.

The genius of John Cannell
*(Inspired artist. Mongol. Confined to an
institution because the experts have measured his brain)*

His fingers
were like deaf ears
and he smelt
of institutions

his eyes
were an old torch
pitted with
corrosion

Red, he said
Green, stabbing
the chalk with
deaf fingers

to make a line
as alive
as Beethoven's
last Quartet.

We believed
he worked so close
because his blind eyes
failed him

but he knew
without knowing
that his heart
could only fall that far.

Diagnosis

I have a Swiss watch
my neighbour's is Japanese
side by side at night
we turn them
like skilled undertakers

our calendar shows
the day strange man died
but does not show
how many
have gone since then

at six o'clock
a photograph
talks about disasters:
we watch and worry
and take our clocks away

we do not understand
why we grow roses
touch each other
and sometimes try
to simulate a storm

we have strong doctors
fast airplanes
and live in layers
like communal graves

there is much death
about us but it is not
our own, therefore
it is not death
and we can describe it

'you will die but I
will not die' is what
we say side by side:
this is our strength
and our civilization

our plague
is the blocked heart
but we are not afraid:
one day we will make
a nursery song
for the photograph
to sing, and then
we will all fall down.

Just before Christmas
(For Len Taylor)

Stunted in Yates's
under a scrounger's stare
he taps our shoulders
to bum a beer

we pay up preferring
to hear the penny drop
then his breath drowning
in thick Mick

but three large burgundies
bring him round again
splashing the same spot
with similar shit

upstairs the piss-
house walls read Lice
in hand-carved lettering:
Fuckoff we tell him

unbreakable he sinks
to where small
pachyderms stink
in London garbage

larger than life
we lurch back
to a boredom too large
for life to catch.

BEACH POEMS
(For Fred, with envy and gratitude)

One.

My daughter is catching shrimps
in the shit from the holiday camp
wherever she looks is only blue
and pale seahorses with pink tails

sometimes she shows me blue
above the roofs of the racked chalets
and we drift into this sunset
in fishing boats with red sails

it is a trick she has which I may
learn, though I have tricks of my own
and one day will teach her how to turn
the sea yellow with strong piss

we make a colourful world: some of my
best friends are green in the afternoon
in the boardroom in snow glowing
from their spines like lost shrimps.

Two.

From the shallows supermarket families
scream each time the bell rings:
this is abandonment where
even the dogs are allowed

at the end of each breakwater
a loud Picasso drags the waves
in smiling and twirls
a monoplane on a long string

he draws a speedboat's blue bow
into a half-erection. 'We like
erections' sing the crowd 'even
in the mornings, pissproud'

the population explodes on this strip
of sand just daring the waves
they are learning what the wind is for
and dreaming that their parents drowned.

Three.

It is an August morning
the semen tide strands two
who gasp, heave and flop back:
they are lost in God

they look only upwards into
his face, where their tails
will smooth a pathway to the top

where the future waits between
striped balls and a steaming urn
and their ancestors are learning
a landscape with brown chips.

Four.

My daughter is catching shrimps
in the shit from the holiday camp
she sees only blue and a pink
seahorse in her muddy net

sometimes she shows me blue
and the pink in her shrimp net
grows into horizons where
she walks and waves me through

I cannot follow her: my love
is limited. I watch her walk
on the seashore by the holiday camp
up to the edge of her pink catch

and when she is stranded at last
on rough sand, my love is
watching God's cruel conjuring
and praying it will work again.

November

Long summer loosens now
the speedboats and the girls depart
shaved stubble shows its skull
and the first mists start
a comfortable loneliness

Dead oaks align themselves
like markers on the marshes
and flat farms, and docile ducks
with winter coughs
sound storybook alarms

Wait. It will happen.
Watch the way the sky expands
not reaching out but running from
small hands freezing as
they squeeze prayer

Behind barns and breakwaters
some corner of the weather
slips to where
the North Sea sways
weed and shingle

Offshore a seal pup barks
and beaches itself upon rough sand
his slashed belly baring
like a broken hand
this year's sacrifice.

Risen sparrow

The June sunshine
in its first day
of full summer
threw a dead sparrow
onto our white patio,
incongruous beside
a fluffy rug and
my leggy daughter

I picked it up
in a gardening glove
and buried it beneath
the prickly pyrecantha,
thinking ashes and dust
worms and the
season's changes

in three days
it will climb from
its dirty hole
and take its place
where I keep
old lives, several
cats and my father

I was ever such
a storer of junk
and quaint stories,
keeping them safe
from June days
in lit gardens
when the sunshine
has its way.

Pastoral

It is no commonplace thing
this East Coast beach where I have heard
Beethoven's cellos reverberating
and my mother shrieking like a seabird

years ago I would sing
skipping a perpendicular suicide
knowing as I crashed God would decide
one-handed to set me back laughing

now he's gone, not dead but slow in middle age
there's no alternative but do the thing yourself
already flying has improved my mother's health
and ghosts are thickening at the sea's edge

I'll set the whole environment in concrete
God left the job half-done in empty air
how else should I excuse a life's defeat
this beach becomes the rush-hour in Trafalgar Square.

Monkey puzzle

Every grandmother
had the three monkeys
on her mantleshelf:

hands over ears
hands over eyes
hands over mouth

and every grandfather
sat in the same chair
with fierce eyes and a riding crop.

In the street outside
the light had no colour at all
no shadows and no colour

and walking from one end to the other
took a whole afternoon
of quite frightening boredom:

why did we live there?
why did my parents visit their parents?
and why did nobody else notice?

hands over ears
hands over eyes
hands over mouth.

Every grandmother
wears a black dress with a funeral smell
every grandfather
wears his skeleton inside loose trousers
and every daughter
wears a pale son to visit them:

the scream of a knife on an empty plate
the rattle of teeth
hands over ears
hands over eyes
hands over mouth.

The light from the street is in here
and it is not possible
to walk to the end of an afternoon:

why do we come here to live?
and why can I not
put my hands across
my ears my eyes and my mouth
in one single gesture?

A late Valentine for Liz

History runs faster than love:
even as you move we are
smothered in old newspapers.

There is no way of understanding this
but when you uncover me each day
soak the pages carefully: there may
be a word still stuck to my flesh.

THREE POSITIONS

1. The chair position (after Keith Vaughan)

In the centre of this room
a chair
in the chair
a man
in the man
a certain position

a position inappropriate
to dancing or dying
but adequate.

White room, white
chair and a man
heavy with himself;

the sky there
almost at a point
where he does not
need the sky

as though God gave
a pattern and left
each one to make
reality.

Chair, room and man
hold each other
like an atom

in a question
of whether to
disturb the world
or masturbate.

2.   The couch position (after Francis Bacon)

Red walls, red couch
and a raw figure
as though the flood
had just gone.

Looking in on edges
which cannot contain
where we flow
into red walls
red couch and meat.

Along the street
clean traffic goes
lights blink on
and a dog barks
for a lost note.

We cannot choose:

looking out we watch
others looking in,
like voyeurs
down the throat
of living.

3.   The bird position (after Paul Klee)

I have said
I will make things
this way

I am not good
at this kind of
statement

am more likely
to eat paint
than paint precisely

would rather cry
at music
than describe it.

The craftsmanship
of God
is his mystery

saying this
I know
it is not enough

yet I say
I will make things
this way

as though God
on his eighth day
will make a reason.

Inheritance

The mummies
were our Saturday treat
and we saved them till last

took in first
the Iron Maiden
the stuffed owls
and the suit of armour
on a plaster horse

then at the end of a corridor
of lighted fishtanks
stood and frightened ourselves
with the long bandaged limb
and its tarry head.

If you spent the night here
you'd be mad by morning:
this we knew as surely
as summer holidays and winter fogs.

Two things bothered me:
why they were called mummies
and what wounded flesh I'd find
if I stripped the cloth away.

Unbandaging myself today
I knew the answers:

as I peeled my mother
from my hands and feet
the white flesh looked
the same but had no feeling

and scraping the usual smile
from its round mirror
I counted those who had
spent the night there
and been mad by morning.

Vocations

Bishop Hughes rises
in Southwark
to face his God:
Do with me what you will
he says, and thus
wise in humility
walks through London;

the bricks sing
for Bishop Hughes, the
bruises on boys' knees
burst into bloom and
meeting the poor, the sick
and the imprisoned he sees
goodness, truth and beauty.

Everything, says Bishop Hughes
is God's will being done
it is necessary
only to remain open.

Regularly in the same suburb
another rises
with night in his eyes:
he vomits, his bowels surge
and thus realized
he walks into London;

the bricks build
sickness on him, he
is imprisoned in
a small room to
train the animals
from his mouth
to devour him.

Everything, says the man
is God's will being done,
having found Him
face to face
in the digestive tract
of a dead sheep.

Nursery Rhyme
(For Nick and Andrea)

Red head and
    white head
upstairs and
    down
your mother was
    an idiot
your father was
    a clown
your childhood was
    a rainy day
your rainbows were
    denied
your mother gave
    the game away
your father sat
    and cried.

Red head and
　　white head
playing in
　　the street
no-one noticed
　　that your shoes
were smaller than
　　your feet
no-one knew the
　　teddy bear
you cuddled in
　　your bed
was bruised about
　　the body
and broken in
　　the head.

Red head and
　　white head
dragging through
　　the years
daily you will
　　curse us
with blasphemies
　　of tears
to wash away the
　　memory
of fairy tales
　　that died
when mother gave
　　the game away
and father sat
　　and cried.

Note on 'Five Ways to Kill a Battery Hen'

There are poems and there are anthology-poems. And a case could be made for arguing that a poet's reputation among the middlebrow reading public depends upon the number and quality of his poems which become anthology-poems. Thus one could argue that Eliot's reputation among middlebrow literates is assured as a cosmopolitan/philosophical/analytical poet because his most anthologized poem is 'The Waste Land,' and that it will remain a 'big' reputation because 'The Waste Land' is a long poem. Auden's reputation among the same people will be that of a sophisticated, amusing social commentator because that is the nature of those early poems which are still his most anthologized pieces.

We like labels and perhaps, in a society as complex as ours, they are necessary if we are to learn anything about anything, but it is interesting to speculate how a poem becomes an anthology-poem. There is, I'm sure, nothing profound about it: it arises out of the laziness of those people who edit anthologies. Most anthologies, I believe, come about because someone in an academic milieu believes his career would be enhanced by having a book in the library with his name on the spine. This imaginary person, lacking the incentive, drive, or industry to write an original book, decides that his ends will be just as well served by editing an anthology. Instead of having something to say through his choice of poems, an individual viewpoint depending upon a wide reading, he goes for his sources to other anthologies and merely reshuffles the poems he finds there. Thus, once you have an anthology-poem, it will appear again and again in other anthologies, achieving a kind of robot life of its own.

Two of my own poems have achieved this robot-anthology-life: 'Five Ways to Kill a Man' and 'Song of the Battery Hen.' So much so that if I am introduced at a party as Edwin Brock, I get a blank look, whereas if I am introduced as the author of one of these two poems, the bell rings and the eyelashes flutter. As the years go by, this becomes more irritating than flattering, and it was in an attempt to get my own back on these two Frankenstein poems that I wrote 'Five Ways to Kill a Battery Hen.'